Cowboy

Songs, Jokes, Lingo 'n Lore

by

Wayne Erbsen

*"You can never tell which
way the pickle's goin' to squirt"*

Order No. NGB400   ISBN 1-883206-06-5

CONTENTS

The Big Corral 6
Bravest Cowboy 7
Bury Me Not on the Lone Prairie 8
The Colorado Trail..10
Cowboy Jack 12
Cowboy's Dream 14
The Cowboy Valentine 16
Devil and the Deep Blue Sea 18
Doney Gal 20
The Girl I Left Behind Me 22
Git Along Little Dogies 24
The Gol-Darned Wheel 26
Goodbye Old Paint 28
The Hills of Mexico 30
Home on The Range 32
I Ride an Old Paint 34
I'm Going to Leave Old Texas 36
Night Herding Song.. 38
The Old Chisholm Trail 40
The Railroad Corral 42
Red River Valley.. 44
The Roving Cowboy 46
Rye Whiskey 47
The Strawberry Roan 48
The Streets of Lorado 50
The Texas Rangers 52
The Trail to Mexico 54
Tying a Knots in the Devil's Tail.......................... 56
When The Work's All Done This Fall 58
Zebra Dun.. 60
Cowboy Lingo..62

Cowboy Insult #1
He couldn't track a bed-wagon through a bog hole.

Howdy!

**Welcome old pard!
You sure am a sight.
I hain't seen you since 'fore daylight.
Climb on down and cool yer saddle.
Chuck's near ready so don't skedaddle.**

S tep in closer to the campfire there stranger so's I can see your brand. Get you some coffee; it's good 'n hot. It ain't none of that sissy coffee. This here coffee'll buck you off if'n you don't hold on tight to the saddle horn. We're startin' our evening campfire and some of the boys have some tall ones to tell and a few songs to sing. Someone might even "agitate the cat-guts" with a tune on a banjo or fiddle. Pull up a stump and join us. Now it's *your* turn to sing one. *Me???* Why, sure. We have a little rule around here that everyone has to sing some kind of a song or tell a tale when it comes their turn. Throw your lasso around a good'n and sing it big and loud. You say you can't sing?? Ha! That's even better! A real cowhand didn't have a good voice, and that never stopped 'em! Just open up your trap and bellow out a good one. Watch it, though...the coyotes might get jealous.

SINGIN' TO 'EM

"His voice sounded like someone forgot to grease the wagon."

C owboys sang. They sang of long days and short nights. They sang of wild broncs, whiskey, and of pals gone on to the prairie in the sky.

Besides being sung for pleasure, songs were tools of the working cowboy. Night herding cowboys either sang, whistled, hummed or spoke to soothe a jumpy herd which might otherwise stampede at the striking of a match or the snapping of a twig. The practice of singing to the night herd became so common that night herding itself became known as "Singin' to 'Em."

Rare was a puncher who knew the tune to the songs he was singin'. Mostly, he grabbed the first tune that came to mind, which might be a hymn remembered from a church hymnal or perhaps a popular ditty heard at a dancehall in some faraway town. When a puncher ran out of words to sing, he just made 'em up. Some of these words would burn a hole in this page were we to print them. The cattle didn't seem to object. They showed their appreciation mainly by waving their tails or wiggling their ears.

Early cowboy songs were seldom, if ever, written down. This changed in 1908 when Jack Thorpe published his *Songs of the Cowboys* and in 1910 when John A. Lomax published *Cowboy Songs and Other Frontier Ballads.* Lomax's book became the unofficial 'bible' for cowboy singers. Many a forgetful puncher reached in a saddlebag or in the back of a chuck wagon for a dog-eared copy of Lomax's book to help recall the words to some half-forgotten song.

SINGIN' TO 'EM

If nothing else, old-time cowboys had a keen sense of humor. Sometimes it was only their humor that got them through droughts and floods, stampedes and stubborn cattle. The quality of a cowboy's singing voice provided many moments of glee for mischievous cowboys. Here are several choice quotes rustled mostly from Ramon F. Adams.

One cowboy was asked if he could sing. "No," he answered, "But sometimes I open my mouth and noise comes out."

His singing was as exciting as a snail climbin' a slick log.

One cowboy sang so good the coyotes gathered and laid off howling to listen.

He had an E-String voice that sounded like a rusty gate hinge.

His singing sounded like the long drawd squeak of a slow- runnin' windmill cryin' for oil.

He had a voice like a scrub bull in a canebreak in cocklebur season.

A cowboy's singin' made the cook stop the chuck wagon to look for a dry axle.

He sang like he was garglin' his throat with axle grease.

He sang that song as quiet as a thief in a chicken house.

Some singers were accused of singing in a "coyote key."

His singin was enough to make a she-wolf jealous.

His voice don't sound like a Christmas chime.

He had a voice like a burro with a bad cold.

He couldn't pack a tune in a corked jug.

Cowboy Insult #2
He was ugly as a burnt boot.

THE BIG CORRAL

"A faint heart never filled a flush."

Poking fun at a roundup cook was about as wise as cozying up to a coiled rattlesnake. Yet that's precisely the theme of the devil-may-care song known as *The Big Corral*. Though widely accepted as a traditional cowboy song, it was actually thrown together in 1922 by Romaine Lowdermilk, with help from Brooks Copeland and Jack Widener. It borrowed the tune of the 1911 gospel song *Press Along to Gloryland* written by James Rowe and Emmett S. Dean.

That ug-ly brute from the cat-tle chute, Press a-long to the big cor-ral. He should be brand-ed on the snoot, Press a-long to the big cor-ral.

CHORUS

Press a-long cow-boy, Press a-long with a cow-boy yell. Press a-long with a noise, big noise, Press a-long to the big cor-ral.

Early in the morning 'bout half-past four,
Press along to the Big Corral.
You'll hear him open his face to roar,
Press along to the Big Corral.

The wrangler's out a-combing the hills,
Press along to the Big Corral.
So jump in your britches and grease up your gills,
Press along to the Big Corral.

The chuck we get ain't fit to eat,
Press along to the Big Corral.
There's rocks in the beans and sand in the meat,
Press along to the Big Corral.

BRAVEST COWBOY

Adapted & Arranged by Wayne Erbsen • Copyright © 1994 • Fracas Music Co. BMI

"Never try to influence a man against his inclination when he is hungry."

Bravest Cowboy wears several hats, including *Sporting Cowboy, The Moundsvilles Prisoner, Seven Long Years in Prison, The Moonshiner's Dream,* and *Dallas County Jail.* Though not a cowboy, this version was put together from the singing of Tommy Jarrell. I rearranged the first verse into a chorus.

I am the brav-est cow-boy, That ev-er rode the West. I've
been all o-ver the Rock-ies, Got bul-lets in my chest.

In eighteen hundred and sixty-three,
I joined the immigrant band.
We marched from San Antonio
Down by the Rio Grande.

I went out on the prairie,
And learned to rob and steal.
And when I robbed that cowboy
How happy I did feel.

I went out on the prairie,
I learned to throw the line.
I learned to pocket money
But I did not dress so fine.

I wore a wide brimmed high hat,
My saddle too was fine.
And when I courted that pretty girl
You bet I called her mine.

I courted her for beauty,
Her love it was in vain.
'Til they carried me down to Dallas
To wear the ball and chain.

> *A cowboy was complaining to a waiter that his steak wasn't cooked enough: "Waiter, do you call this well-done? I've seen critters hurt worse than this get well."* [1]

Cowboy Insult #3
His mustache smelled like a mildewed saddle blanket after it had been rid on a soreback hoss three hundred miles in August.

BURY ME NOT ON THE LONE PRAIRIE

"All a man needs is a rope, a running iron, and the nerve to use it."

*B*ury Me Not on the Lone Prairie was so common among the cowboys that even their horses nickered it and coyotes howled it. The song was actually based on a much earlier poem written by Edwin Hubbell Chapin, who was a Universalist clergyman in Boston. He published "The Ocean Buried," as a poem in *Southern Literary Magazine* in 1839. The first song version was published as sheet music in 1850 as *The Ocean Burial* with music attributed to George N. Allen. However, one song collector wrote that *The Ocean Burial* was sung to the old air *Hind Horne.* Apparently, some unknown sailor gave up his sea legs and took to cowboyin'. Somewhere along the line he changed *The Ocean Burial* to *Bury Me Not on the Lone Prairie.*

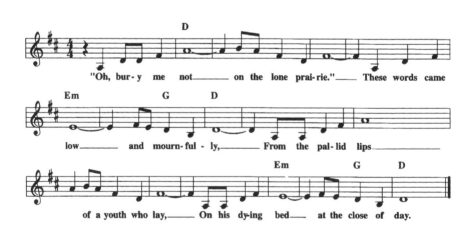

"Oh, bur-y me not___ on the lone prai-rie."___ These words came low___ and mourn-ful-ly,___ From the pal-lid lips___ of a youth who lay,___ On his dy-ing bed__ at the close of day.

Cowboy Insult #4
His family tree was a shrub.

(continued)

He has wasted and pined till o'er his brow
Death's shades were slowly gathering now.
He thought of home and loved ones nigh,
As the cowboys gathered to watch him die.

"Oh bury me not on the lone prairie,
Where the coyotes howl and the wind blows free.
In a narrow grave just six by three-
Oh bury me not on the lone prairie."

"It matters not, I've oft been told,
Where the body lies when the heart grows cold.
Yet grant, oh grant, this wish to me,
Oh bury me not on the lone prairie."

"I wish to lie where a mother's prayer
And a sister's tear will mingle there,
Where friends can come and weep o'er me.
Oh bury me not on the lone prairie."

> *A cowboy once made the mistake of arguing with a trapper over whether wildcats had long tails or not. The trapper settled the argument by furnishing as his proof a Colt .45 revolver. The coroner's decision was that any Hombre who was crazy enough to call a long-haired, whisky-drinking trapper a liar had died of ignorance.* [2]

"For there's another whose tears will shed
For the one who lies in a prairie bed.
It breaks my heart to think of her now,
She has curled these locks; she had kissed this brow."

"Oh bury me not..." but his voice failed there.
We took no heed to his dying prayer.
In a narrow grave, just six by three,
We buried him there on the lone prairie.

And the cowboys now as they roam the plain,
For they marked the spot where his bones were lain,
Fling a handful of roses o'er his grave
With a prayer to God his soul to save.

Drinkin' Water
"The water is a little thick an' you may have to chew it a little before you swallow it, but it's dern good water." [3]

THE COLORADO TRAIL

"When a bad man dies he either goes to hell or to the Pecos."

**Strap on your chaps, boys, and tie on your slicker;
Before the day's over, you'll wish you had some licker.**

*T*he Colorado Trail was originally composed by James A. Bliss and quickly became a favorite of the cowboys. It was often sung as lonesome as a preacher on payday night. The author added the last two verses.

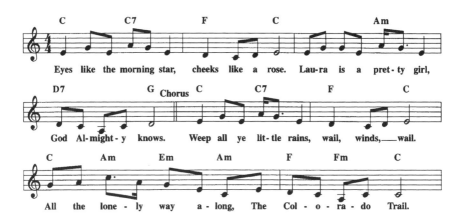

Eyes like the morning star, cheeks like a rose. Lau-ra is a pret-ty girl, God Al-might-y knows. Weep all ye lit-tle rains, wail, winds, —— wail. All the lone-ly way a-long, The Col-o-ra-do Trail.

The herd it stretches on and on,
Through an endless night.
I'll sing to them a lonesome song,
'til the morning light.

Lonesome days and sleepless nights,
Have lost all their charms.
I wish that I was back at home,
Safe within your arms.

A cowboy checked into a big city hotel, and was shocked at the charge of $2.50 for his room. He finally conceded to pay such an outlandish price, but when the porter tried to lead him into an elevator, he stopped dead in his tracks.

"No sir! he said. "I ain't gonna pay $2.50 for no little dinky room such as that." [4]

Cold!!!

On a cold midwinter day, an Indian and a cowboy were traveling together. It was colder than a well-chain in December. The Indian had on no clothing except a loincloth and a blanket. The cowboy had on red flannel underwear, woolen shirt, heavy pants, jacket, and overcoat. Yet through all this clothing, the wind cut like a knife. The Indian showed no signs of discomfort.

"Aren't you cold?" asked the cowboy.

"No," said the Indian.

"I don't understand it. Here I am wrapped up with all the clothes I can carry and I am about to freeze to death. And you have on only a thin blanket and you say you are not cold."

"Is your face cold?" asked the Indian.

"No, my face is not cold, but I'm about frozen everywhere else."

"Me all face," said the Indian. [5]

COWBOY JACK

"A change of pasture can make the calf fatter."

*C*owboy Jack is a sorrowful ballad set to an equally mournful melody. Its ancestors include *Your Mother Still Prays For You Jack*, which in turn was based on the old English ballad *Lord Lovel.* The earliest known recordings of *Cowboy Jack* were by Jack Mathis (1928) for Columbia, Peg Morland (1929) for Victor and The Arkansas Woodchopper (1930) for Conqueror. In 1934 the song was recorded on Bluebird both by the Carter Family and by The Girls of the Golden West.

He was just a lone - ly cow - boy____ With a heart so

brave and true.____ And he learned to love a

maid - en____ With eyes of heav - en's blue.____

Cowboy Fishin'

A cowboy went fishing and caught a fifty pound catfish. Not wanting to eat it, he started to throw it back in the water when another cowboy produced a red hot branding iron. Together, they branded the catfish with the bridle bit brand, just in case any other fishermen might try to claim it as part of their herd.

COWBOY JACK

(continued)

They learned to love each other,
And had named their wedding day.
When a quarrel came between them,
And Jack he rode away.

He joined a band of cowboys,
And tried to forget her name.
But out on the lone prairie,
She waits for him the same.

One night when work was finished,
Just at the close of day,
Someone said, "Sing a song, Jack,
To drive dull cares away."

When Jack began his singing,
His mind did wander back.
For he sang of a maiden
Who waited for her Jack.

> *Folks don't mind if you tell lies, just so's you're sincere.*[6]

"Your sweetheart waits for you, Jack,
Your sweetheart waits for you.
Out on the lonely prairie
Where the skies are always blue."

Jack left the camp next morning,
Breathing his sweetheart's name.
"I'll go and ask forgiveness,
For I know that I'm to blame."

But when he reached the prairie,
He found a new made mound.
And his friends they sadly told him,
They'd laid his loved one down.

They said as she was dying,
She breathed her sweetheart's name.
And asked them with her last breath,
To tell him when he came:

"Your sweetheart waits for you, Jack,
Your sweetheart waits for you.
Out on the lonely prairie,
Where the skies are always blue."

Cowboy Insult #5
He ain't fit to shoot at when you want to unload and clean yo' gun.

COWBOY'S DREAM

"Kickin' never gets you nowhere, 'less'n you're a mule."

Cowboy work was dangerous work. Between stampeding cattle and attacks by Indians, brushes with death were frequent. Many wondered whether a cowboy would go to that great roundup in the sky or forever be stuck eating the dust of the devil's herd. Since churches were "as rare as sunflowers on a Christmas tree" and "Sunday stopped at the Missouri River," *Cowboy's Dream* was a favorite starting in the mid-1870's among the cowboys wondering about their fate.

As to who actually wrote *Cowboy's Dream,* we have as much chance as a snowball in Hell in finding its true composer. As many as eight men solemnly claimed authorship. To add to the confusion, the song goes under at least thirteen different titles.

We do know for sure that it was first recorded in 1924 by Charles Nabell on Okeh 40252-B under the title *The Great Round-Up.* It is sung to the tune of *My Bonnie Lies Over the Ocean* and makes a mighty pretty song.

14

Cowboy's Dream

(continued)

The eastern lady who was all ready to take a horseback ride said to the cowboy, "Can you get me a nice gentle pony?" "Shore," said the cowboy. "What kind of a saddle do you want, English or western?" "What's the difference?" asked the lady. "The western saddle has a horn on it," said the cowboy. "If the traffic is so thick here in the mountains that I need a horn on my saddle, I don't believe I want to ride." [7]

The road to that bright mystic region
Is a dim narrow trail, so they say.
But the broad one that leads to perdition
Is posted and blazed all the way.

They say there will be a great roundup,
When cowboys like dogies will stand.
To be marked by the Riders of Judgement,
Who are posted and know every brand.

I wonder if ever a cowboy,
Prepared for that great judgement day
Could say the Boss of the Riders:
"I'm ready, come drive me away."

They say He will never forget you,
That He knows every action and look.
So for safety, you'd better get branded,
Get your name in that Great Tally Book.

I know there are many stray cowboys,
Who'll be lost in that great final sale.
When they might have gone on to green pastures,
Had they known of the dim, narrow trail.

For they're all like the cows that are locoed,
That stampede at the sight of a hand.
And are dragged with a rope to the roundup,
And get marked with a crooked man's brand.

They tell of another Big Owner,
Who is ne'er overstocked, so they say.
And who always makes room for the sinner,
Who strays from the straight, narrow way.

Cowboy Insult #6
He was so dumb he couldn't drive nails in a snowbank.

THE COWBOY VALENTINE

"It's the man that's the cowhand, not the outfit he wears."

Here's a new song based on two rare occurrences for an old-time cowboy: getting an armload of roses as a Valentine gift, and getting all dressed up to go courtin'. To see Jake, you'd think he was spraddled up like a Mexican revenue officer at a Christmas ball.

Now, old Jake Wooley was an ornery old cuss, As mean as a side-wind-er slither-in' in the dust. But he took a fan-cy to old Spin ster Brown, so he roped up his cay-use and rode in-to town.— With his hair— slicked down and his whisk-ers all combed, He smells as sweet as the day he was born. He's all gus-sied up and his boots ev-en shined, He's a walk-ing bou-quet, just a cow-boy valen-tine.

Chorus

Cowboy Insult #7
He don't know as much about it as a hog does a sidesaddle.

THE COWBOY VALENTINE

(continued)

Jake slipped into town so the boys never knowd,
That he's courtin' this lady, yeah, he's courtin' her slow.
A bump on her nose and a wart on her chin,
Her head's like a beehive with the top all caved in.

Jake summoned his courage and heads for her door,
Never expecting what she had in store.
An armload of roses she gave him to say,
That she loved this cowboy on Valentine's day.

Well, the boys had a fit, yes they hooted and yelled,
When they saw old Jake ridin' far over the dell.
With an armload of roses as red as the clay,
That was given to him on this Valentine's day.

A Few Uses For a Neck Scarf [8]

Ankle Support ✦ Arm Sling ✦ Bag ✦ Bandage ✦ Basket ✦ Bathing Suit ✦ Belt ✦ Breech Cloth ✦ Bridle ✦ Dish Cloth ✦ Dust Mask ✦ Ear Muffs ✦ Fish Line ✦ Fish Net ✦ Flag ✦ Gunsling ✦ Handcuff ✦ Handkerchief ✦ Hat ✦ Hobble ✦ Mail Bag ✦ Napkin ✦ Note Paper ✦ Ruler ✦ Sack ✦ Sling Shot ✦ Sponge ✦ Strainer ✦ Towel ✦ Tourniquet ✦ Trail Marker ✦ Weapon ✦ Whip.

UGLY??

*One time there was a cowhand named Tollie Sands who was so ugly he had to sneak up on a dipper to get a drink of water. Once, he purchased a mirror from a traveling peddler but wisely kept it hid so his jealous wife wouldn't see him admiring himself. One time his wife was snooping in Tollie's stuff and to her horror, she discovered the mirror. "So **that's** the sour-faced hussy you've been chasin,' is it?" With that, she smashed the mirror over Tollie's bald head.* [9]

17

DEVIL AND THE DEEP BLUE SEA

"A wink's as good as a nod to a blind mule."

Here's a song about a feller in one heck of a fix. The tune was inspired by the beautiful Texas waltz, *Midnight on the Water*, which in turn was inspired by the version of *Goodbye Old Paint* recorded in 1947 by Jess Morgan for John Lomax.

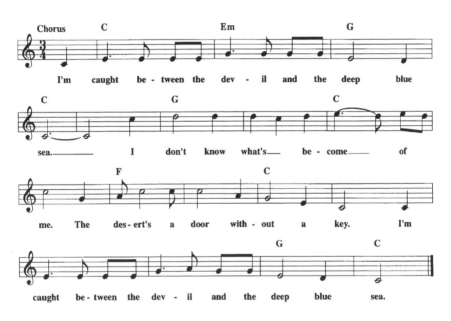

Chorus

I'm caught be-tween the dev-il and the deep blue sea. I don't know what's be-come of me. The des-ert's a door with-out a key. I'm caught be-tween the dev-il and the deep blue sea.

Cowboy Insult #8
He knows as much about it as a hog does a hip pocket in a bathing suit.

DEVIL AND THE DEEP BLUE SEA

(continued)

If the desert were a man with lines on his face,
I'd hit him up for a handout or a new grubsteak.
If the desert were a song with words that ran free,
I'd sing myself away from this country.

If I could tell a whopper that would sure enough come true,
I'd tell myself a big one about the likes of me and you.
How we bet against a dealer who was cheatin' on the sly,
When I raked up all my winnings we could drink the heavens dry.

Sittin' 'round the firelight eatin' a can of beans,
With a saddle for a pillow in the moonlight's gleam.
A bellyfull of grub helps a man to forget,
I'm outnumbered by the coyotes and the buzzards overhead.

DONEY GAL

"The wilder the colt, the better the hoss."

A cowboy without his horse was about as natural as a trout without his water. The bond between man and horse is caught in *Doney Gal,* one of my personal favorites. The doney gal was a cowboy's horse, but in frontier days in the southern mountains, a doney gal was a sweetheart. The word "doney" doubtless derived from the Spanish word "doña" meaning "woman." The last three verses were made up by the author.

We ride the range from sun to sun, For a cow-boy's work is nev-er done. We're up and gone at the break of day, Driv-ing the do-gies on their wea-ry way. It's rain or shine, sleet or snow, Me and my Don-ey Gal are bound to go. Yes, rain or shine, sleet or snow, Me and my Don-ey Gal are on the go.

DONEY GAL

(continued)

Grub Calls

- ❖ *Grub pile, come a-runnin' fellers*
- ❖ *Swaller an' git out.*
- ❖ *Grab it now, or I'll spit in the skillet*
- ❖ *Boneheads, boneheads, take it away*
- ❖ *Grab a plate an' growl*
- ❖ *Grab 'er boys or I'll throw 'er out*
- ❖ *Shut yo' eyes an' paw 'er over*
- ❖ *Here's hell, boys!* [10]

A cowboy's life is a dreary thing,
It's rope, and brand and ride, and sing.
Day or night in the rain or hail,
We'll stay with the dogies out on the trail.

Tired and hungry, far from home,
I'm just a poor cowboy and bound to roam.
Starless nights and lightning glare,
Danger and darkness everywhere.

Drifting my Doney Gal round and round,
Steers are asleep on a new bed ground.
Riding night herd all night long,
Singing softly a cowboy song.

Swimming rivers along the way,
Pushing for the North Star day by day.
Storm clouds break, and at breakneck speed,
We follow the steers in a wild stampede.

A cowboy's song on a cheap guitar,
Out on the prairie where there ain't no bars.
Makes me think of my younger days,
When I spent all my money at the Lady Gaye.

We're up and we're gone before daybreak,
Leading them dogies all along their way.
My pony's tired, his feet are sore,
But he'll take his rest on Heaven's shore.

At evening's end round the firelight's glow,
We'll tell the tales of long ago.
Of gals so sweet they'd make you sigh,
And no one cares if you're telling lies.

A cowboy was drinking at a bar when his boss came in and told him that he had been raised an extra ten dollars a month.
"Th' heck!" said the cowboy. "I hain't even drunk up last month's pay yet. That extra ten dollars'll kill me fo' sure." [11]

THE GIRL I LEFT BEHIND ME

"When in doubt, trust your hoss."

*T*he Girl I Left Behind Me has been a popular ditty that dates back to around 1758-59 in England, when it was also known as *Brighton Camp* or *Blyth Camps.* Early versions were played on fife and drum as military marches and later to accompany English country dances. Unlike most tunes, the melody of *The Girl I Left Behind Me* has steadfastly resisted change, while various sets of words have attached to it.

Traveling to the colonies with early settlers, *The Girl I Left Behind Me* was popular both in the Revolutionary War and the Civil War and was a favorite with General George A. Custer and his Seventh Calvary. Country fiddlers eventually took up the tune and played it for square dances and quadrilles.

This cowboy version rode out West on horseback and in covered wagons and was corralled by John A. Lomax who led it into his 1910 book *Cowboy Songs and Other Frontier Ballads.* I learned it from Jim Bob Tinsley who didn't leave his girl (Dottie) behind him, but took her with him!

THE GIRL I LEFT BEHIND ME

(continued)

If ever I get off the trail,
And the Indians don't find me,
I'll go right back where I belong,
To the girl I left behind me.

The night was dark and the cattle run,
With the boys coming on behind me,
My mind went back at my pistol's crack,
To the girl I left behind me.

The wind did blow, the rain did flow,
The hail did fall and blind me.
And I thought of her, that sweet little girl,
The girl I left behind me.

She wrote ahead to the place I said,
And I was glad to find it.
She said, "I'm true, when you get through,
Ride back and you will find me."

When we sold out, I took the train,
I knew where I could find her.
When I got back we had a smack,
And I'm no gol-durned liar.

Lingo for Holding the Saddle Horn:

- *Chokin' the horn*
- *Clawin' Leather*
- *Grabbin' the Nubbin'*
- *Grabbin' the Post*
- *Pullin' Leather*
- *Reachin' for the Apple*
- *Shakin' Hands With Grandma*
- *Squeezin' the Biscuit*
- *Squeezin' Lizzie*
- *Huntin' Leather.* [3]

Sometimes cowboys referred to beans as "Deceitful Beans" because they talked behind your back. [10]

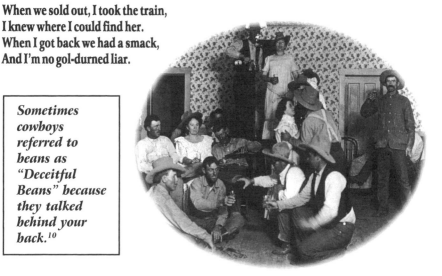

Cowboy Insult #9
He don't know dung from wild honey.

GIT ALONG LITTLE DOGIES

"A cow outfit's never better than its hosses."

Whoopee-Tie-Yi-Yo, Git Along Little Dogies was collected not from a lariat-swinging cowboy, but a guitar-strumming gypsy fortune teller in Fort Worth, Texas. Its origins have been traced at least as far back as 1672 to an English broadside ballad entitled *I Father a Child That's None of My Own*. The word "dogie" is not, as some think, an offshoot of "doggie," meaning a small dog. Rather, it refers to an orphaned calf who is forced by hunger to eat grass before it can digest it properly. Such a calf's belly usually swells, giving it the nickname "doughguts," "doughies," or "dogies."

As I was a-walkin' one morn-ing for pleas-ure, I spied a cow-punch-er a-rid-in' a-long. His hat was throwed back and his spurs were a jin-glin', And as he ap-proached he was sing-ing this song.

Chorus

Whoop-ee ti yi yo, Git a-long, lit-tle do-gies, It's your mis-for-tune, and none of my own. Whoo-pee ti yi yo, Git a-long, lit-tle do-gies, you know that Wy-o-ming will be your new home.

(continued)

Names of Cowboy Horses

Red Hell • Tar Baby • Sail-Away Brown • Big Henry • Streak • Leapin' Lena • Old Sardine • Sugar Dip • Dough Gut • Old Slick • Hammer Head • Churn Head • Lightnin' • Apron Face • Feathers • Panther • Leather Lip • Knot Belly • Milk Shake • Old Guts • Widow Maker • Molasses Mouth • Diamond Eye • Pickle Simon • Anytime • Mountain Sprout • Chub • Dumbell • Rambler • Powder • Straight Edge • Snake Eye • Peanuts • Shide Poke • Gotch Ear • Gold Dollar • Popcorn • Bootjack • Whiskey Pete • Sassy Sam.[3]

Early in the springtime we round up the dogies,
Mark 'em, and brand 'em, and bob off their tail;
Round up the horses, load up the chuck wagon,
Then throw the little dogies out on the long trail.

Night comes on and we hold 'em on the bed ground.
The same little dogies that rolled on so slow.
We rolled up the herd and cut out the stray ones,
Then roll the little dogies like never before.

Some boys go up the long trail for pleasure.
But that's where they get it most awfully wrong.
For you'll never know the trouble they give us,
As we go driving the dogies along.

Your mama was raised away down in Texas,
Where the jimson weeds and sandburs grow.
We'll fill you up on prickly pear and cholla,
Then throw you on the trail to Idaho.

Cowboy Insult #10
He didn't have nuthin' under his hat but hair.

THE GOL-DARNED WHEEL

"You can never tell which way the pickle's goin' to squirt."

Cowboys bravely faced blizzards, buzzards, bucking bron-
cos and Brahma bulls without flinching. But one cowboy
met his match when he stumbled upon a tenderfoot's
bicycle which he called "The Gol-Darned Wheel." The unknown wordsmith who composed this hilarious tale sure had a
way with words. To sing it, your tongue better be saddlebroke
so's you can spit out the words without getting tangled up as a
tenderfoot in a lariat.

I can rope and throw a long-horn of the wild-est Tex-as brand. And at
In-dian dis-a-gree-ments I can take a lead-ing hand. But I
final-ly met my mas-ter and he real-ly made me squeal. When the
boys got me a-strad-dle of that gol-darned___ wheel.

'Twas a tenderfoot who brought it while he was on his way
From this land of freedom out to San Francisco Bay.
He tied it at the ranch house for to get outside a meal,
Never thinkin' we would monkey with his gol-darned wheel.

Arizona Jim begun it when he said to Jack McGill
He said that I'd been bragging way too much about my skill.
They said I'd find myself against a different kind of deal
If I would get astraddle of that gol-darned wheel.

Cowboy Insult #11
His brain cavity wouldn't make a drinkin' cup for a canary bird.

THE GOL-DARNED WHEEL

(continued)

Such a slam against my talent made me madder than a mink,
And I swore that I would ride it for amusement or for chink.
That it was just a plaything for the kids and such about,
And they'd have their ideas shattered if they'd lead the critter out.

They held it while I mounted and I gave the word to go.
The shove they gave to start warn't unreasonably slow,
But I never spilt a cussword and I never give a squeal,
I was building reputation on that gol-darned wheel.

Holy Moses and the Prophets, how we split the Texas air,
And the wind it made whip-crackers of my same old canthy hair.
And I sorta comprehended as down the hill we went,
There was bound to be a smash-up that I couldn't well prevent.

Oh, how them punchers bawled, "Stay with her, Uncle Bill!
Stick your spurs in her, you sucker! turn her muzzle up the hill!"
But I never made an answer, I just let the cusses squeal,
I was building reputation on that gol-darned wheel.

> *Lingo for a*
> *Cowboy's*
> *Bed:*
> * *Lay*
> * *Hot Roll*
> * *Velvet Couch*
> * *Shake Down*
> * *Crumb*
>   *Incubator*
> * *Hen Skins*
> * *Flea-trap.* [3]

> *Two cowboys were eating a meal in a restaurant. One said: "The butter's so strong it could walk over and say howdy to the coffee." His pal answered: "Well, if it did, the coffee's too weak to answer back."* [11]

The grade was mighty sloping from the ranch down to the creek,
And I went a-gallyflutin' like a crazy lightning streak,
Just a-whizzing and a-dartin', first to this way and then that,
The darned contrivance wobbling like the flying of a bat.

I pulled up on the handles but I couldn't check it up,
I yanked and sawed and hollered, but the darn thing wouldn't stop.
And then a sort of meechin' in my brain began to steal,
That the Devil held a mortgage on that gol-darned wheel.

I've a sort of dim and hazy remembrance of the stop,
With the world a-goin' round and the stars all tangled up.
Then there came an intermission that lasted till I found,
I was lying at the bunkhouse with the boys all gathered round.

And a doctor was a-sewing on the skin where it was ripped,
And old Arizona whispered, "Well, old boy, I guess you're whipped."
I said that "I am busted from sombrero down to heel."
He grinned and said, "You ort to see that gol-darned wheel!"

GOODBYE OLD PAINT

"Color don't count if the horse don't trot."

Whoever put together *Goodbye Old Paint* left only a very faint trail for us to follow, and most of that's been blown away by the prairie wind. More than likely, it was composed out of pieces of many other songs which bummed a ride on the back of *Goodbye Old Paint.* Some of these hitchhikers included *Jack of Diamonds, Rye Whiskey, The Rebel Soldier, Clinch Mountain, Texas Cowboy, My Horses Ain't Hungry, The Inconstant Lover* and *Sioux Indians.* We have Texas cowboy Jess Morris to thank for preserving the song by singing it into John A. Lomax's recording contraption in 1947. Morris not only sang a great version of it but also fiddled the hound out of it, leaving other fiddlers to drool.

GOODBYE OLD PAINT

(continued)

Old Paint's a good pony, he paces when he can,
Goodbye little doney, I'm off to Montan'.

Go hitch up your horses and feed 'em some hay,
An' set yourself by me as long as you'll stay.

We spread down the blanket on the green grassy ground,
While the horses and cattle were a-grazing around.

My horses ain't hungry, they won't eat your hay,
My wagon is loaded and rollin' away.

My foot's in the stirrup, my bridle's in hand,
Goodbye little Annie, my horses won't stand.

The last time I saw her was late in the fall,
She was ridin' Old Paint and a-leadin' Old Ball.

Cheap!!?

One cowboy was so cheap he went into a general store and insisted on buying just one spur. When the shopkeeper protested against breaking up a set, the cowboy swore that where one side of his horse went, the other side was sure to follow.

Cowboy Insult #12
He was as shy of brains as a terrapin is of feathers.

THE HILLS OF MEXICO

"A cork screw never pulled a man out of a hole."

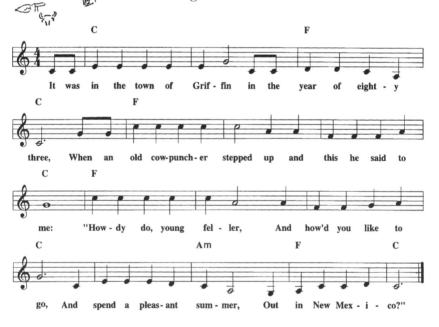

Here is a song that cowboys used to entertain each other with around the campfire late of an evening. Since the songs were sung from memory, sometimes it took the whole crew to recall (or make up) all the verses to longer ballads like this one. The cowboys must have extracted a certain amount of glee in singing the verse about the foreman: "We left his bones to bleach upon the hills of Mexico."

The Hills of Mexico is some cowboy's version of the popular frontier ballad, *The Buffalo Skinners,* which in turn was based on the English ballad *The Caledonia Garland.*

It was in the town of Grif-fin in the year of eight-y three, When an old cow-punch-er stepped up and this he said to me: "How-dy do, young fel-ler, And how'd you like to go, And spend a pleas-ant sum-mer, Out in New Mex-i-co?"

Cowboy Insult #13
He's as crazy as popcorn on a hot stove.

THE HILLS OF MEXICO

(continued)

I, being out of employment to this puncher I did say:
"Depends upon the wages that you will have to pay.
You pay to me good wages and transportation too,
And I think that I will go with you one summer season through."

We left the town of Griffin in the merry month of May.
The flowers were all blooming and everything seemed gay.
Our trip it was a pleasure, the road we had to go
Until we reached Old Boggy out in New Mexico.

It was there our pleasures ended and troubles then begun.
The first hailstorm came on us, oh how those cattle run!
Through mesquite, thorns, and thickets we cowboys had to go,
While the Indians watched our pickets out in New Mexico.

And when the drive was over, the foreman wouldn't pay.
To all of you good people this much I have to say:
"With guns and rifles in our hands, I'll have you all to know.
We left his bones to bleach upon the hills of Mexico."

And now the drive is over and homeward we are bound.
No more in this damned old country will ever I be found.
Back to friends and loved ones and tell them not to go.
To the God-forsaken country they call New Mexico.

> ### Lingo for Bucking:
> - *Boiled Over*
> - *Broke in Two*
> - *Came Apart*
> - *Folded Up*
> - *Kettled*
> - *Shot its Back*
> - *Slatted its Sails*
> - *Unwound*
> - *Hopped for Mama*
> - *Wrinkled His Spine.*[3]

HOME ON THE RANGE

"Wide open spaces don't breed no chatterboxes."

*H*ome on the Range was the first cowboy song I ever heard. I was amazed how anyone could even write a song like this. Apparently, a lot of other people wondered the same thing. In fact, the song was the center of a $500,000 lawsuit as to its authorship in the 1930's. Samuel Moanfeldt was hired to find the truth about the origin of *Home on the Range.* He discovered that it was first published as the poem *Western Home* in 1873 as written by Dr. Brewster Higley. Higley was well known as an eccentric Kansas physician. Credit for setting it to music went to his neighbor, Dan Kelley, who had fought in the Civil War.

(continued)

Where the air is so pure, the zephyrs so free,
And the breezes so balmy and light.
Then I would not exchange my home on the range
For all of your cities so bright.

The red man was pressed from this part of the West,
And he's likely no more to return
To the banks of Red River, where seldom, if ever,
Their flickering campfires burn.

How often at night when the heavens are bright,
With the light from the glittering stars.
Here I stood there amazed, and asked as I gazed,
If their glory exceeds that of ours.

A cowboy was urging his buddy to go with him to a traveling stage show to see a concert singer.
"Is she any good?" he was asked.
"Good, why man, she's a virtuoso!"
"To heck with her morals," the waddie snorted. "I just want to know if she can sing." [12]

One cowboy earned the nickname "Dishwater" when he stumbled out of his bedroll one night and mistook the camp cook's dishwater for the water bucket. [10]

I love the wild flowers in this dear land of ours,
And the curlew I love to hear scream.
I love the wild rocks and the antelope flocks,
That graze on the mountaintops green.

Oh give me a land where the bright diamond sand,
Flows leisurely down the stream.
Where the graceful white swan goes sliding along,
Like a maid in a heavenly dream.

Cowboy Insult #14
He couldn't hit the ground with his hat in three throws.

I RIDE AN OLD PAINT

"Tossin' your rope before buildin' a loop don't ketch the calf."

I Ride an Old Paint is among the most well-known of all the cowboy songs. Carl Sandburg learned it from Margaret Larkin of Las Vegas, New Mexico. She first heard it sung by a cowboy in Santa Fe who was last seen leaving for the Mexican border.

I ride an old paint,— I lead an old Dan.— I'm off to Mon - tan' for to throw the hoo - li - han. They feed in the cou - lees, they wa - ter in the draw; Their tails are all mat - ted, their backs are all raw.

CHORUS
Ride a - round lit - tle do - gies, ride a - round them— slow, For the fier - y and snuf-fy are a - rar - in' to go.

I RIDE AN OLD PAINT

(continued)

Old Bill Jones had two daughters and a song,
One went to Denver, and the other went wrong.
His wife, she died in a poolroom fight,
And he sings this song from morning till night.

Oh, when I die, take my saddle from the wall,
Put it on my pony and lead him from the stall.
Tie my bones to his back, turn our faces to the west,
And we'll ride the prairies we love the best.

A tenderfoot was lost, but was relieved to see a cowhand riding toward him. "How far is it to town?" he shouted to the cowhand. "'Bout a half quart down the trail," answered the drunk cowboy.

A Guide to the Lingo

Paint horses were also called "pinto," "piebald," "pied," "calico," or "skewbald" and were kin to Indian ponies. Most were very strong and tough, but never attained much size. The word "pinto" comes from the Spanish word "pintar," which means "to paint."

A "hoolihan" is a loop thrown clockwise to rope a horse. When roping a wild cow, a good horse will stop in its tracks, causing the creature on the other end of the rope to hit the ground faster than you can spit and holler howdy! "Firey" and "Snuffy" refer to wild or spirited cattle.

I'm Going to Leave Old Texas

"Montana for bronco riders & hoss thieves, Texas for ropers & rustlers."

I'm Going to Leave Old Texas answers to several names including *Old Texas, The Texas Song, Texas Cowboy* and *An Old Cowman's Lament.* The melody is nearly identical to the second half of *The Trail to Mexico.*

I'm going to leave old Texas now,
They've got no use for the long-horn cow.

They've plowed and fenced my cattle range,
And the people here all seem so strange.

I'll take my horse; I'll take my rope,
And hit the trail upon a lope.

I'll say adios to the Alamo,
And turn my face toward Mexico.

The hard, hard ground will be my bed,
And my saddle seat will hold my head.

And when my ride on earth is done,
I'll take my turn with the Holy One.

Yet in that far off cattleland,
I sometimes acted like a man.

And so my friends, I'll bid adieu,
I'm a better man for knowing you.

I'm going to leave old Texas now,
They've got no use for the longhorn cow.

A Camp Cook's Rules

- ✓ IF YOU CAN'T WASH DISHES, DON'T EAT.
- ✓ WE USE WOOD IN THE COOKSTOVE CUT 16" LONG BUT NO LONGER
- ✓ A BUSY COOK LOVES A FULL WOOD BOX.
- ✓ A FULL WATER BUCKET MAKES A HAPPY COOK
- ✓ STRAY MEN ARE NOT EXEMPT FROM HELPING WASH DISHES, BRINGING WOOD OR WATER
- ✓ THE WELL IS JUST 110 STEPS FROM THE KITCHEN, MOSTLY DOWNHILL BOTH WAYS [13]

Cowboy Insult #15
His face was puckered like wet sheepskin before a hot fire.

A Cowboy Jingle

Carnation milk advertised in stock papers a prize for the best jingle praising its product. One ranch woman composed a jingle that went:

> *Carnation milk, best in the lan',*
> *Comes to the table in a little red can.*

When she finished it, she asked one of the cowboys to mail it on his way through town. Some weeks later she received a curt letter from Carnation warning her about sending in an unsavory jingle. Perplexed, she started suspecting the cowboy of doctoring her jingle. Once accused, the cowboy freely confessed to adding a few lines "Jes' to give it a little more punch:"

> *Carnation milk, best in the lan'.*
> *Comes to the table in a little red can.*
> *No teats to pull, no hay to pitch,*
> *Jes' punch a hole in the son-of-a_____.[10]*

NIGHT HERDING SONG

"Any hoss's tail kin ketch cockleburs."

Most of the songs made up on night herd were forgotten as soon as they left the puncher's lips. *The Night Herding Song*, composed by Harry Stephens, had a different fate. He managed to write it down while pulling a sixteen hour shift herding wild horses in Yellowstone Park at forty dollars a month around 1909.

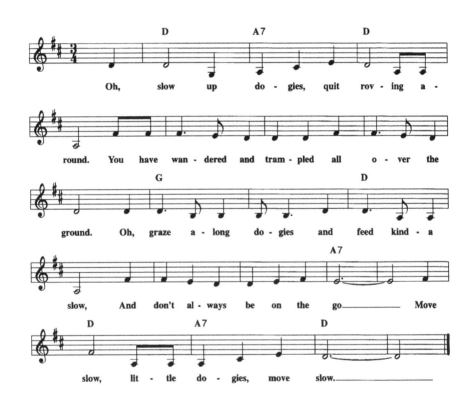

Oh, slow up do - gies, quit rov - ing a - round. You have wan - dered and tram - pled all o - ver the ground. Oh, graze a - long do - gies and feed kind - a slow, And don't al - ways be on the go___ Move slow, lit - tle do - gies, move slow.___

Cowboy Insult #16
He can't tell skunks from house cats.

Night Herding Song

(continued)

I've circle-herded, trail-herded, night-herded too,
But to keep you together that's what I can't do.
My horse is leg-weary and I'm awful tired,
But if I let you get away I'm sure to get fired.
Bunch up, little dogies, bunch up.

Oh, say little dogies, when you gonna lay down,
And quit this forever a-shifting around?
My limbs are weary and my seat is all sore,
Lay down, dogies, like you laid down before-
Lay down, little dogies, lay down.

Lay still little dogies, since you have laid down,
And stretch away out on the big open ground.
Snore loud little dogies, and drown the wild sound,
They'll all go away when the day rolls around-
Lay still, little dogies, lay still.

John Cox's new wife, Eda May, had never been to town. One time John had to go to town to get a haircut and a shave and Eda May naturally went along. They checked into a hotel but Eda May decided to stay put in the room. For safety, John locked the door from the outside, and took the key.

Going downstairs, John was jumped by some old cowpuncher buddies, who hauled him off to the bar and to the biggest poker game he'd ever been in. John was soon facing the biggest winning streak he ever had run into. The game lasted way into the night, and on into the next afternoon. John had a stack of chips in front of him so high he could hardly see over the top and one of the biggest jackpots of the game was lying on the table. John stayed with a pair of queens then drew three cards, and got the other two queens. The sight of so many women in one hand reminded him of Eda May. All of a sudden, John jumped up, knocking over all the chips and headed for the door.

"Wait," the others yelled. "You can't quit now."

"If there's anythin' left of me in fifteen minutes, boys," John promised, "I'll be back. I done left Eda May locked up in a room for twenty-four hours an' I ain't neither fed nor watered her!" [9]

THE OLD CHISHOLM TRAIL

"Only a fool argues with a skunk, a mule, or a cook."

*T*he *Old Chisholm Trail* was a genuine favorite of the cowboys. There was hardly a waddie who didn't add a verse or two to it. Some argued that if you laid the verses down end to end you could walk all the way from San Antonio to Dodge City without ever touching dirt. Most punchers considered it a matter of pride to add to the trail of verses. One claimed to know eighty-nine verses while another swore there were thousands. The more whiskey, the more verses.

Well come a-long boys and lis-ten to my tale, I'll

CHORUS

tell you of my trou-bles on the old Chisholm Trail, Come-a ti - yi - yip- pee yip - pee yea, yip - pee yea, Come - a ti - yi yip - pee yip - pee yea!

On a ten dollar horse and a forty dollar saddle,
I started out to punchin' them longhorn cattle.

I started up the trail October twenty-third,
I started up the trail with the 2U herd.

I'm up in the morning before daylight,
And before I sleep the moon shines bright.

It's bacon and beans most every day,
We'll soon be a-eatin' prairie hay.

With my seat in the saddle and my hand on the horn,
I'm the best damned cowboy that ever was born

It's cloudy in the west and a-lookin' like rain,
And my damned old slicker's in the wagon again.

THE OLD CHISHOLM TRAIL

(continued)

A stray in the herd and the boss said, "Kill it!"
So I shot it in the rump with the handle of a skillet.

I woke one morning on the old Chisholm Trail,
With a rope in my hand and a cow by the tail.

Old Ben Bold was a blamed good boss,
But he'd go to see the girls on a soreback hoss.

Last time I saw him he was going 'cross the level,
A-kickin' up his heels and a-running like the devil.

Last night on guard when the leader broke ranks,
I jumped on my horse and spurred him in the flanks.

Thirsty??

Two cowhands saved their money and bought a town's only saloon. After a week the thirsty gathered in front of the closed saloon.

"When you goin' to open this place up?" yelled one of the dry natives.

"Open, hell," answered the new saloon owner. "We bought this joint for our own drinkin'." [14]

The wind began to blow and the rain began to fall,
It looked by damn like we was gonna lose them all.

Me and Old Blue Dog arrived on the spot,
And we put 'em to milkin' like the boiling of a pot.

No chaps, no slicker, and it's pourin down rain,
I swear I'll never night herd again.

I crippled my horse and I don't know how,
A-ropin' at the horns of a 2U cow.

I went to the boss to draw my roll,
And he had me figured nine dollars in the hole,

Me and my boss we had a little spat,
So I hit him in the face with my ten-gallon hat.

I'll sell my horse and I'll sell my saddle,
You can go to hell with your longhorn cattle!

With my knees in the saddle and my seat in the sky,
I'll quit punchin' cows in the sweet by-and-by.

Cowboy Insult #17
She's so ugly, she could back a buzzard off a gut-wagon.

THE RAILROAD CORRAL

"A full house divided don't win no pots."

*T*he Railroad Corral is one of a small handful of cowboy songs that has a known composer. It was written by Joseph Mills Hanson and first published in "Frank Leslie's Monthly Magazine" in 1904. He wrote it to the tune of the Scottish ballad *Bonnie Dundee*. The first half of the melody also favors the melody of *Rye Whiskey, Jack of Diamonds, Clinch Mountain* and *The Rabble Soldier.*

We're up in the morn - ing at break - ing of day. The chuck wa - gon's bu - sy, the flap - jacks in play. The herd is a - stir o - ver hill - side and vale, With the night rid - ers crowd- ing them on - to the trail.

Chorus:

Come take up your cinches and shake out your reins,
Come wake your old bronco and break for the plains.
Come roust out your steers from the long chaparral,
For the outfit is off to the railroad corral.

Cowboy Insult #18

He was so ugly he had to sneak up on a dipper to get a drink of water.

THE RAILROAD CORRAL

(continued)

The sun circles upward, the steers as they plod,
Are pounding to power the hot prairie sod.
And it seems, as the dust makes you dizzy and sick,
That we'll never reach noon and the cool shady creek.

But tie up your kerchief and ply up your nag,
Come dry up your grumbles and try not to lag.
Come drive out your steers from the long chaparral,
For we're far on the road to the railroad corral.

The afternoon shadows are starting to lean,
When the chuck wagon sticks in a marshy ravine.
The herd scatters farther than vision can look,
You can bet all the punchers will help out the cook.

Come shake out your rawhide and shake it up fair,
Come break your old bronco and take in your share.
Come roust out your steers from the long chaparral,
For it's all in the drive to the railroad corral.

But the longest of days must reach evening at last,
The hills are all climbed and the creeks are all passed.
The tired herd droops in the yellowing light;
Let 'em loaf if they will, for the railroad corral.

So flap up your holster and snap up your belt,
And strap up your saddle whose lap you have felt.
Good-bye to the steers from the long chaparral,
There's a town that's a trump by the railroad corral.

> *A cowboy who considered himself a tough customer took things too far one time. He boarded a train one day without a ticket. When the conductor asked him for his fare, the cowboy pulled his six gun and declared that it was all the ticket he needed. The conductor left but returned presently with a rifle which he stuck under the cowboy's nose.*
>
> *"Your ticket has just expired, Mister," he announced and signaled for the train to stop. He let the cowboy off miles from nowhere, and one cowboy learned the advantage of paying his fare before boarding a train."* [15]

RED RIVER VALLEY

"You can judge a man by the hoss he rides."

Red River Valley is a national treasure that's probably been sung around more campfires than any song in America. Though American as s'mores and corn-on-the-cob, its beginnings lie not in the Red River of Texas and Oklahoma but in the Red River section of Canada. Cowboy music historian Jim Bob Tinsley has found evidence that *Red River Valley* was written by Jethro de la Roche for Amaryllis Milligan in the late 1860's.

From this val - ley they say you are go - ing,_____ I will miss your bright eyes and sweet smile.____ For they say you are tak-ing the sun- shine_____ That has bright-ened our path - way a - while.____

Chorus:
Come and sit by my side if you love me.
Do not hasten to bid me adieu.
But remember the Red River Valley,
And the cowboy that loves you so true.

Cowboy Insult #19
He was so fat, you'd have to throw a diamond hitch to keep him in the saddle.

(continued)

I've been waiting a long time my darling,
For the sweet words you never would say.
Now at last all my fond hopes have vanished,
For they say you are going away.

Oh there never could be such a longing,
In the heart of a poor cowboy's breast.
That now dwells in the heart you are breaking,
As I wait in my home in the West.

Do you think of the valley you're leaving?
Oh how lonely and drear it will be!
Do you think of the kind heart you're breaking,
And the pain you are causing to me?

As you go to your home by the ocean,
May you never forget those sweet hours.
That we spent in the Red River Valley,
And the love we exchanged mid the flowers.

> *There was once an old-time cowhand who ordered some toilet paper from a mail-order catalog. They wrote back and requested that he look in his catalog to give them the exact order number. He answered 'em right back and told them that if he had their catalog, he sure wouldn't need the toilet paper.*

THE ROVING COWBOY

Adapted & Arranged by Wayne Erbsen • Copyright © 1995 Fracas Music Co. BMI

"A pat on the back don't cure saddle gals."

*T*he Roving Cowboy has a spooky melody and is based on the old English ballad widely known as *The Girl I Left Behind*. This version combines the chorus as sung by Buell Kazee on Brunswick 156-A with the verses collected by Glen Ohrlin in his book "Hell-Bound Train."

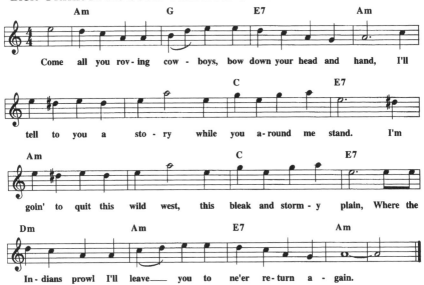

Come all you rov-ing cow-boys, bow down your head and hand, I'll
tell to you a sto-ry while you a-round me stand. I'm
goin' to quit this wild west, this bleak and storm-y plain, Where the
In-dians prowl I'll leave— you to ne'er re-turn a-gain.

My mother's hand did tremble, said son, "Oh son, I fear,
Some accident may happen, I'll never see you here.
Oh, may the Lord go with you wherever you may roam,
And send this wandering cowboy back to his native home."

A girl so sweet and lovely drew closer to my side,
And promised me so faithfully that she would be my bride.
I kissed away the flowing tears that filled her deep blue eyes.
I'll ne'er forget the girl I love until the day I die.

I've tried the trails of rambling, and rambling I know well,
I've crossed the Rocky Mountains, where many a brave boy fell.
I've been in the great Southwest with Apaches fierce and wild,
I'll ne'er forget the girl I love or see a sweeter smile.

RYE WHISKEY

"Never drink unless you're alone or with somebody."

Distant kin to *Rye Whiskey* are scattered far and wide and go under such aliases as *Jack of Diamonds, The Rebel Soldier, Clinch Mountain, My Horses Ain't Hungry* and *If the River Was Whiskey.* The earliest ancestors have even appeared in a London play in 1734 with these lines: "He eats when he's hungry, and drinks when he's dry/ And down, when he's weary, contented does lie."

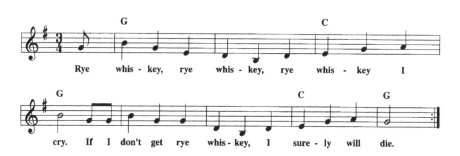

Rye whis-key, rye whis-key, rye whis-key I cry. If I don't get rye whis-key, I sure-ly will die.

Oh whiskey you villain,
You've been my downfall.
You've beat me, you've banged me,
But I love you for all.

Jack of Diamonds, Jack of Diamonds,
I know you of old.
You've robbed my poor pockets
Of silver and gold.

If the ocean was whiskey,
And I was a duck,
I'd dive to the bottom
And never come up.

But the ocean ain't whiskey,
And I ain't a duck,
So I'll round up the cattle
And then I'll get drunk.

I'll drink my own whiskey,
I'll drink my own wine,
Some ten thousand bottles,
I've killed in my time.

I'll drink and I'll gamble,
My money's my own,
And them that don't like it
Can leave me alone.

My foot's in the stirrup,
My bridle's in my hand,
I'm leaving sweet Molly,
The fairest in the land.

Her parents don't like me,
They say I'm too poor,
They say I'm unworthy
To enter her door.

THE STRAWBERRY ROAN

"Polishing your pants on saddle leather don't make you a rider."

The Strawberry Roan, by Curley W. Fletcher, is the most popular cowboy song about a wild bucking horse. Fletcher had been a mule skinner, prospector, musician, magazine editor, author and poet. He first published it in the Arizona Record on December 15, 1915 as *The Outlaw Broncho*. Two years later he reworked it and published it in a slim book called *Rhymes of the Roundup*, which he hawked at western rodeos.

I gets all excited and asks what he pays
To ride that old horse for a couple of days.
He offers me ten, and I says, "I'm your man,
'Cause the horse hasn't lived that I couldn't fan."

THE STRAWBERRY ROAN

(continued)

He says, "Git your saddle, and I'll give you a chance."
So we climb in the buckboard and ride to the ranch.
Early next morning right after chuck
I go down to see if this outlaw can buck.
There in the corral just a-standing alone
Is a scrawny old pony—a strawberry roan.
He has little pig eyes and a big Roman nose,
Long spavined legs that turn in at the toes.

Little pin ears that are split at the tip,
And a 44 brand there upon his left hip.
I put on my spurs and I coil up my twine,
And says to the stranger, "That ten-spot is mine."
Then I put on the blinds and it sure is a fight.
My saddle comes next, and I screw it down tight.
Then I pile on his back and well I know then,
If I ride this old pony, I'll sure earn my ten.

> **Oink!!**
> *One cowboy ate so much hog belly that he grunted in his sleep and was afraid to take off his pants for fear he'd sprouted a curly tail.*

Cowgirl Nicknames

- ❖ *Calamity Jane*
- ❖ *Gar-Face Nell*
- ❖ *Jack Rabbit Sue*
- ❖ *Virgin Mary*
- ❖ *Bronco Jane*
- ❖ *Frog-Lip*
- ❖ *Pitchin' Sal*
- ❖ *Four-Ace Flora*
- ❖ *Buffalo*
- ❖ *Heifer*
- ❖ *Society Mary*
- ❖ *Wingless Angel*
- ❖ *Rantin' Nell*
- ❖ *Razorback Molly*
- ❖ *Covered Wagon Liz*
- ❖ *Dodge City Kate* [3]

For he bows his old neck and he leaps from the ground,
Ten circles he makes before he comes down.
He's the worse bucking bronco I've seen on the range,
He can turn on a nickel and give you some change.
He goes up again and he turns round and round,
As if he's quit living down there on the ground.
He turns his old belly right up to the sun;
He sure is a-sunfishing son-of-a-gun.

He goes up in the East and comes down in the West.
To stay in the saddle, I'm doin' my best.
I lose both my stirrups and also my hat,
And start pullin' leather as blind as a bat.
He goes up once more, and he goes way up high,
And leaves me a-settin' up there in the sky.
I turn over twice and I come down to earth,
And I start into cussin' the day of his birth.

I've rode lots of ponies out here on the range,
And there's been one or two that I shore couldn't tame.
But I'll bet all my money there's no man alive,
Can ride that old horse when he makes his high dive.

THE STREETS OF LAREDO

"Every man is entitled to scratch his own itch."

The Streets of Laredo, also known as *The Cowboy's Lament*, has a lineage as long as your arm and then some. It has been traced to the Irish ballad *The Unfortunate Rake*, which tells the tale of a poor lad who contracted a "social disease." The song was popular in about 1790.

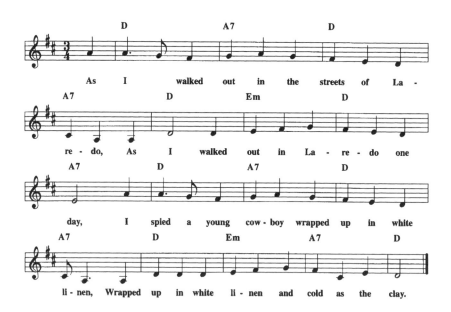

As I walked out in the streets of La-re-do, As I walked out in La-re-do one day, I spied a young cow-boy wrapped up in white li-nen, Wrapped up in white li-nen and cold as the clay.

Oh beat the drum slowly and play the fife lowly;
Play the Dead March as you carry me along.
Take me to the green valley and lay the sod o'er me,
For I'm a young cowboy and I know I've done wrong.

Cowboy Insult #20
He was so mean, he'd fight a rattler and give him the first bite.

THE STREETS OF LAREDO

(continued)

"I see by your outfit that you are a cowboy."
These words he did say as I boldly stepped by.
"Come sit down beside me and hear my sad story,
I'm shot in the breast and I know I must die."

"My friends and relations they live in the Nation,
They know not where their dear boy has gone.
I first came to Texas and hired to a ranchman,
Oh I'm a young cowboy and I know I've done wrong."

"It was once in the saddle I used to go dashing,
It was once in the saddle I used to go gay.
First to the dram house and then to the card house,
Got shot in the breast and I'm dying today."

Lingo for Whiskey

Bottled Courage • Bug juice • Gut Warmer • Neck Oil • Nose-paint • Wild Mare's Milk • Coffin Varnish • Gut Warmer • Redeye • Scamper Juice • Joy Juice • Snake Pizen • Tonsil Varnish • Tarantula Juice • Firewater • Tornado Juice • Dynamite . [1]

"Get six jolly cowboys to carry my coffin,
Get six pretty maidens to bear up my pall.
Put bunches of roses all over my coffin,
Put roses to deaden the clods as they fall."

"Go gather around you a group of young cowboys,
And tell them the story of this my sad fate.
Tell one and the other, before they go further,
To stop their wild roving before it's too late."

"Go bring me a cup, a cup of cold water,
To cool my parched lips," the young cowboy said.
Before I returned, the spirit had left him,
And gone to its Maker—the cowboy was dead.

We beat the drum slowly and played the fife lowly,
And bitterly wept as we bore him along.
For we all loved our comrade, so brave, young and handsome,
We all loved our comrade although he'd done wrong.

Windy??

It was so windy in Texas one time that a hen setting against the wind layed the same egg five times!

THE TEXAS RANGERS

"Success is the size of the hole a man leaves when he dies."

The Texas Rangers were a tough outfit of lawmen who could "ride like a Mexican, trail like an Indian, shoot like a Tennessean, and fight like the very devil." They struck terror in the hearts of Comanche Indians starting in 1835.

The song known as *The Texas Rangers* tells the chilling tale of a battle with the Indians on the Texas frontier. It was written during or just after the Civil War and published in 1874 in F.D. Allan's *Lone Star Ballads*. The song has been attributed to a fifteen year old soldier of the Arizona Brigade.

Come all you Tex - as Ran - gers, where - ev - er you may be, I'll tell you of some trou - bles, that hap - pened un - to me. My name is noth - ing ex - tra, so that I will not tell, But here's to all good ran - gers, I'm sure I wish you well.

Cowboy Insult #21
He was mean enough to eat off the same plate with a snake.

When at the age of sixteen, I joined a jolly band.
We marched from San Antonio down to the Rio Grande.
Our captain he informed us, perhaps he thought it right,
"Before we reach the station, we'll surely have to fight."

I saw the smoke ascending, it seemed to reach the sky.
The first thought that came to me, "My time has come to die!"
I thought of my dear mother, in tears to me did say:
"To you they are all strangers, with me you'd better stay."

I saw the Indians coming, I heard their awful yell.
My feelings at that moment, no human tongue can tell.
I saw their glittering lances, their arrows around me flew,
'til all my strength had left me and all my courage too.

We fought for nine full hours before the strife was o'er.
The likes of dead and dying, I've never seen before.
And when the sun had risen, the Indians they had fled.
We loaded up our rifles and counted up our dead.

Now all of us were wounded, our noble captain slain.
And when the sun was shining across the bloody plain.
Six of the noblest rangers that ever roamed the West
Were buried by their comrades with arrows in their breasts.

Perhaps you have a mother, likewise a sister too.
Perhaps you have a sweetheart, to weep and mourn for you.
If this be your position, although you'd like to roam.
I'll tell you from experience, you'd better stay at home.

Calls to Gently Awaken Slumbering Cowhands

Wake up, Jacob!
Day's a-breaking! Peas in the pot,
And the hoecakes a-baking!

Wake up, snakes! Day's a-breaking!
Wake up snakes and bite a biscuit!

Roll out, roll out while she's hot!

Bacon in the pan,
Coffee in the pot;
Get up and get it--
Get while it's hot.

If you can't get up,
There are men in Dodge
that can.[16]

The Trail to Mexico

"You can't tell how far a bullfrog'll jump by the size of its feet."

The old English songs that had a hankering for life in the New World had to be pretty tough hombres. The weaker ones succumbed to sea sickness and scurvy aboard crowded and often leaky sailing vessels. The tough or lucky ones might live long enough to be carried West in covered wagon, by horseback or on foot. Such was the fate of *The Trail to Mexico*. It started out as early as 1694 bearing the ponderous title *The Seaman's Complaint for his Unkind Mistress of Wapping*. Later versions were spotted in Edinburg, Scotland in 1739 under the alias *The Disappointed Sailor*. It was also collected as *Early, Early in the Spring*. Take Carl Sandburg's advice in singing the song: "Get the hang of the tune and all the lines are easy to pucker in."

I made up my mind to change my way, To leave the crowd that was too gay, And leave my native home a-while And travel west for many a mile.

All About Cowchips

Camp cooks were notoriously "techy." Among their aggravations was the scarcity of good firewood out on the prairie. Resourceful cooks relied on cowchips which also became known as "compressed hay," "prairie pancakes," "surface coal," "squaw wood," "cow wood" and "prairie coal." When dry, they did make a hot fire. Though chips gave off an unsavory odor, burning them did not affect the food. One old range cook who used his hat for a bellows claimed that in one season he "wore out three good hats tryin' to get the damned things to burn." [3]

THE TRAIL TO MEXICO

(continued)

It was in the merry month of May
When I started for Texas far away.
I left my darling girl behind
She said her heart was only mine.

When I embraced her in my arms,
I thought she had ten thousand
  charms.
Her caresses soft, her kisses sweet
Saying "We'll get married next time
  we meet."

It was in the year of '83,
That A.J. Stinson hired me.
He said, "Young man, I want you to go
And follow my herd into Mexico."

Well it was early in the year,
When I volunteered to drive the steers.
I can tell you boys, it was lonesome go
As the herd rolled on toward Mexico.

When I arrived in Mexico,
I longed for my girl, but I could not go.
So I wrote a letter to my dear
But not a word did I ever hear.

I started back to my once loved home.
Inquired for the girl I called my own.
They said she'd married a richer life
"Therefore, cowboy, seek another wife."

"Oh curse your gold and your silver too.
Oh curse the girls that don't prove true.
I'll go right back to the Rio Grande
And get me a job with a cowboy band."

She said, "Oh buddy, please stay at
home,
Don't be forever on the roam
There's many a girl more true than I,
So don't go where the bullets fly."

"I know girls more true than you,
And I know girls who would prove true.
But I'll go back where the bullets fly
And follow the cow trail 'til I die."

> ### *Recipe for Cowboy Coffee*
> *Take two pounds of Arbuckle's coffee, put in 'nough water to wet it down, boil it for two hours, then throw in a hoss shoe. If the hoss shoe sinks, she ain't ready.[10]*

Cowboy Insult #22
He's so crooked, he could swaller nails an' spit out corkscrews.

TYING KNOTS IN THE DEVIL'S TAIL

"The man that straddles the fence usually has a sore crotch."

T*ying Knots in the Devil's Tail* is a frolicsome song about two drunk cowboys and their run-in with the devil himself. It was written by Gail I. Gardner as a poem called "The Sierry Petes" aboard a Santa Fe train in 1917.

D

A——— way up high in the Sier - ry Petes, Where the

A7

yel - low pines grow tall, Sand - y Bob and

D

Bus - ter Jiggs, Had a ro - deer camp last fall.

Oh, they'd taken their hosses and runnin' irons
And mabbe a dawg or two,
An' 'lowed they'd brand all the long-yered calves,
That come within their view.
And any old dogie that flapped long yeres,
An' didn't bush up by day,
Got his long yeres whittled an' his old hide scorched,
In a most artistic way.

Now one fine day ole Sandy Bob,
He throwed his seago down,
I'm sick of the smell of burnin' hair,
And I 'lows I'm a-goin' to town.
So they saddles up an' hits 'em a lope,
Fer it warn't no sight of a ride,
And them were the days when a Buckaroo
Could ile up his insides.

TYING KNOTS IN THE DEVIL'S TAIL
(continued)

Oh, they starts her in at the Kaintucky Bar,
At the head of whiskey Row,
And they'd winds up down by the Depot House
Some forty drinks below.
They then sets up and turns around,
And goes her the other way,
An' to tell you the Gawd-forsaken truth,
Them boys got stewed that day.
As they were a-ridin' back to camp,
A-packin' a pretty good load,
Who should they meet but the Devil himself,
A-prancin' down the road.
Sez he, "You ornery cowboy skunks,
You'd better hunt yer holes,
Fer I've come up from Hell's Rim Rock,
To gather in yer souls."

Sez Sandy Bob, "Old Devil be damned,
We boys is kinda tight,
But you ain't a-goin' to gather no cowboy souls,
'Thout you has some kind of a fight."
So Sandy Bob punched a hole in his rope,
And he swang her straight and true,
He lapped it on to the Devil's horns,
An' he taken his dallies too.
Now Buster Jig was a riata man,
With his gut-line coiled up neat,
So he shaken her out an' he built him a loop,
And he lasses the Devil's hind feet.
Oh, they stretched him out an' they tailed him down,
While the irons was a-gettin hot,
They cropped and swaller-forked his yeres,
Then they branded him up a lot.

They pruned him up with a de-hornin' saw,
And knotted his tail fer a joke,
They then rode off and left him there
Necked to a Black-Jack oak.
If you're ever up high in the Sierry Petes,
An' you hear one Hell of a wail,
You'll know it's that Devil a-bellerin' around,
About them knots in his tail.

Cowboy Camp Rule

Complain about the cooking...You become the cook.

One night a cowboy grimaced over the sourdough he was trying to eat and said, "Such sinkers! Burnt on the bottom, soggy in the middle, and salty as hell!" Seeing the hopeful expression on the cook's face, he quickly added: "Hell, that's jes' the way I like 'em." [14]

WHEN THE WORK'S ALL DONE THIS FALL

"There ain't much paw an' beller to a cowboy."

*W*hen the Work's All Done This Fall is a favorite sentimental cowboy ballad based on the death of the cowboy Charlie Rutledge. It was written as a poem in 1893 by D. J. O'Malley and first set to the tune of *After The Ball* by Charles W. Harris. Sometime later the song acquired the tune it now carries. It was first recorded for Victor in 1925 by Carl Sprague, and sold over 900,000 copies.

A group of jol-ly cow-boys, dis-cuss-ing plans at ease, Says one, "I'll tell you some-thing boys, if you will lis-ten please. I am an old cow-punch-er, and here I'm dressed in rags; I used to be a tough one, and go on great big jags.

Cowboy Insult #23
He was so lazy, molasses wouldn't run down his legs.

WHEN THE WORK'S ALL DONE THIS FALL

(continued)

"But I have got a home boys, and a good one you all know,
Although I haven't seen it since long, long ago.
I'm going back to Dixie once more to see them all,
I'm going to see my mother when the work's all done this fall."

"When I left my home boys, my mother for me cried,
She begged me not to go boys, for me she would have died.
My mother's heart is breaking, breaking for me that's all,
And with God's help I'll see her when the work's all done this fall."

That very night this cowboy went out to stand his guard;
The night was dark and cloudy and storming very hard.
The cattle, they got frightened, and rushed in wild stampede,
The cowboy tried to head them, while riding at full speed.

While riding in the darkness, so loudly did he shout,
Trying his best to head them and turn the herd about.
His saddle horse did stumble and on him it did fall,
Now he won't see his mother when the work's all done this fall.

His body was so mangled, the boys all thought him dead,
They picked him up so gently and laid him on a bed.
He opened wide his blue eyes, and looking all around,
He motioned to his comrades to sit near on the ground.

"Boys, send mother my wages, the wages I have earned,
For I am so afraid boys, the last steer I have turned.
I'm going to a new range, I hear my Master's call.
And I'll not see my mother when the work's all done this fall."

"Fred you take my saddle; George, you take my bed,
Bill you take my pistol after I am dead.
Then please think of me kindly when you look upon them all,
For I'll not see my mother when the work's all done this fall."

Poor Charlie was buried at sunrise, no tombstone at his head,
Nothing but a little board, and this is what it said:
"Charlie died at daybreak, he died from a fall.
And he'll not see his mother when the work's all done this fall."

"All this country needs," said a newcomer near Fort Smith, Arkansas, "is a little more water, and a better class of people to move in." A cowboy from Oklahoma grinned. "Yeah," he murmured, "they say that's all Hell needs."[17]

ZEBRA DUN

"The bigger the mouth the better it looks when shut."

*Z*ebra Dun is the humorous song of an educated stranger who rode into a cowboy camp. Thinking him a tenderfoot and wanting some fun, the cowboys offered him breakfast and a fresh mount, which was the wildest bucking bronco they could find. The tenderfoot was not as green as they thought and he soon turned the joke on them.

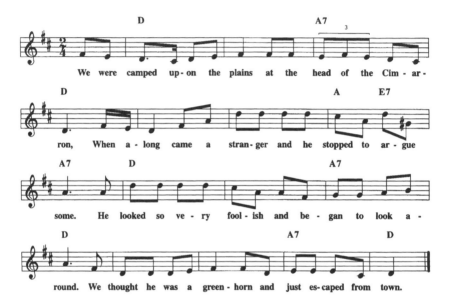

We were camped up-on the plains at the head of the Cim-ar-ron, When a-long came a stran-ger and he stopped to ar-gue some. He looked so ve-ry fool-ish and be-gan to look a-round. We thought he was a green-horn and just es-caped from town.

We asked if he'd had breakfast and he hadn't had a sniff.
We opened up the chuck-box and told him help himself.
He got himself some beefsteak, a biscuit, and some beans,
And then began to talk about the foreign kings and queens.

He talked about the Spanish War and fighting on the seas,
With guns as big as beef steers and ramrods big as trees.
He spoke about old Dewey, the fightin' son of a gun,
He said he was the bravest cuss that ever pulled a gun.

Cowboy Insult #24
He was grittin' his teeth like he could bite the sites off a six-gun.

ZEBRA DUN

(continued)

He said he'd lost his job upon the Santa Fe,
And he was going across the plains to strike the 7D.
He didn't say how come it, some trouble with the boss,
And he said he'd like to borrow a nice fat saddle hoss.

This tickled all the boys to death; they laughed down in their sleeves.
We told him he could have a horse as fresh as he would please.
So Shorty grabbed a lasso and he roped the zebra dun,
Then led him to the stranger and we waited for the fun.

The stranger hit the saddle and old Dunny quit the earth.
He traveled straight up in the air for all that he was worth.
A-pitching and a-squealing and a-having wall-eyed fits.
His hind feet perpendicular and his front ones in the bits.

> *"It don't take near as much water to make coffee as some folks think it does."* [18]

We could see the tops of trees beneath his every jump.
But the stranger he was glued there just like a camel's hump.
He sat there upon him and he curled his black mustache,
Just like a summer boarder a-waiting for his hash.

Camp Cook Names:
Soggy • Pot Russler • Lean Skillet • Old Pud • Coosie • Old Lady • Belly Cheater • Biscuit Roller • Dough Boxer • Dough Puncher • Greasy Belly • Grub Worm • Gut Robber • Sourdough [3]

He thumped him in the shoulders and spurred him when he whirled.
And showed us flunky punchers he's the wolf of this world.
When the stranger had dismounted once again upon the ground,
We knew he was a thoroughbred and not a gent from town.

The boss he was a-standing and watching all the show.
He walked up to the stranger and he told him not to go.
"If you can use the lasso like you rode the zebra dun,
Then you're the man I've looked for ever since the year of One."

Oh, he could use the lasso and he didn't do it slow.
And when the cows stampeded he was always on the go.
There's one thing and a shore thing I've learned since I was born:
That ev'ry educated feller ain't a plumb greenhorn.

61

Ace in the Hole: a hideout, a hidden gun
Acorn Calf: a weak or runty calf
Among the Willows: dodging the law
Arkansas Toothpick: a large knife
Auger: the big boss
Axle Grease: butter
Bad Medicine: bad news
Bait: food
Bake: to overheat a horse
Baldface Dishes: china dishes
Band Wagon: a peddler's wagon
Bangtail: a mustang
Banjo: a miner's term for a short-
 handled shovel
Bar Dog: a bartender
Barefoot: an unshod horse
Bark: to scalp
Barking at a Knot: trying the impossible
Base Burner: a drink of whiskey
Bay: a horse of light-red color
Bean Master: a camp cook
Bear Sign: doughnuts
Bed Ground: where cattle are held
 at night
Bed Him Down: to kill a man
Beef Tea: shallow water where cows
 have stood
Belly Cheater: a cook
Belly Robber: a cook
Belly Through the Brush: dodge the law
Belly Wash: weak coffee
Bending the Elbow: drinking whiskey
Bible: cigarette papers
Big Jump: death
Big Pasture: the penitentiary
Big Sugar: ranch owner
Biscuit: saddle horn
Biscuit Roller: a cook
Biscuit Shooter: a cook
Bite the Ground: to be killed
Black-Eyed Susan: a cowboy's six gun

Black Snake: a long whip
Black Spot: shade
Black Water: weak coffee
Blue Belly: a Yankee
Blue Lightnin': a six gun
Boggy Top: a pie with no top crust
Boil Over: a horse that starts bucking
Bone Orchard: cemetery
Boogered Up: crippled
Boston Dollar: a penny
Brain Tablet: a cigarette
Broken Wind: not what you think
 —a lung infection in horses
Brown Gargle: coffee
Bucket of Blood: a tough saloon
Buffaloed: confused
Bug Juice: whiskey
Bull nurse: a cowboy
Bumblebee Whiskey: whiskey with
 a sting
Burn the Breeze: ride at full speed
Burro Milk: nonsense
Caboodle: the whole thing
Cahoots: partnership
Calf Slobbers: meringue
California Collar: a hangman's noose
California Prayer Book: a deck of cards
Callin': courtin'
Can Openers: spurs
Cash In: to die
Catalog Woman: mail order bride
Catgut: a rope
Cattle Kate: a female cattle rustler
Cat Wagon: a wagon carrying women
 of less than honorable intentions
Chew Gravel: thrown from a horse
Choke Strap: a necktie
Chuck: food
Chuck-Wagon Chicken: bacon
Clean His Plow: beat up in a fight
Cold Meat-Wagon: a hearse

COWBOY LINGO

Coosie: camp cook
Corral Dust: lies and tall tales
Cottonwood Blossom: a man lynched from the limb of a tree
Cowboy Cocktail: straight whiskey
Cow Salve: butter
Crawl his Hump: to start a fight
Crumb Castle: chuck wagon
Crumb Incubator: a cowboy's bed
Curry the Kinks Out: to break a horse
Cut a Rusty: to go courtin'
Cut His Suspenders: a departed cowboy
Desert Canary: a burro
Dice House: bunkhouse
Didn't Have a Tail Feather Left: broke
Diggers: spurs
Ditty: a which-i-ma-call-it
Dive: bunkhouse
Doghouse: bunkhouse
Dough-Belly: cook
Doughgods: biscuits
Down to the Blanket: almost broke
Dream Book: cigarette papers
Dusted: thrown from a horse
Eatin' Irons: knives, forks, and spoons
Equalizer: a pistol
Excuse-me-ma'am: a bump in the road
Fandango: a dance
Fiddle: a horse's head
Fill a Blanket: roll a cigarette
Flannelmouth: a talkative person
Flea Trap: bedroll
Gambler's Ghost: a white mule
Gelding Smacker: a saddle
Getting Long in the Tooth: getting old
Grubworm: cook
Hair in the Butter: a delicate situation
Hot Rock: a biscuit
Lead Plumb: a bullet
Lincoln Skins: greenbacks

Lizzy: saddle horn
Lookin' at a Mule's Tail: plowing
Look-See: to investigate
Lynching Bee: a hanging
Mail-Order Cowboy: a tenderfoot
Mexican Strawberries: dried beans
Monkey Ward Cowboy: a tenderfoot
Mule's Breakfast: a straw bed
Neck Oil: whiskey
Paintin' his Nose: getting drunk
Pair of Overalls: two drinks of whiskey
Play a Lone Hand: do something alone
Pop Skull: whiskey
Porch Percher: a town loafer
Pot Rustler: cook
Prairie Dew: whiskey
Prairie Tenor: coyote
Puddin' Foot: an awkward horse
Put on the Nose Bag: to eat
Round Browns: cow chips
Saddle Bum: a drifter
Sage Hen: a woman
Savvy: knowledge or understanding
Singin' to 'Em: standing night guard
Smoke Wagon: a six gun
Snuffy: a wild or spirited horse
Squeezing the Biscuit: holding the saddle horn
Stretchin' the Blanket: telling a tall tale
Stringing a Whizzer: telling a tall tale
Swamp Seed: rice
Talking Iron: a six shooter
Tear Squeezer: a sad story
Techy as a Teased Snake: grumpy
Texas Cakewalk: a hanging
Too Much Mustard: a braggart
Uncorkin' a Bronc: breaking a horse
Unshucked: draw a gun
War Bonnet: a hat
Wasp Nest: light bread
Whistle Berries: beans

THANKS!

Wranglin' the songs for *Cowboy Songs, Jokes, Lingo 'n Lore* was not a job for one lone puncher. No Sir! It took a whole crew of cowhands to herd the songs to market. First of the cowboys to thank is Jim Bob Tinsley and the Jim Bob Tinsley Museum and Research Center in Brevard, North Carolina. Jim Bob shared his years of research with me both in person and through his great book *He Was Singing This Song*, published by the University Presses of Florida. A great big thanks also goes to cowgirls Shelia Shidnia for musical transcriptions and marketing, to Janet Swell Webb of PageScape Publications for layout and editing, to my wife Barbara Swell for editing and running the chuck wagon, and to Ginger K. Renner and Dianne Keller for tracking down illustrations by Charlie Russell. Thanks to cowpuncher Steve Millard for the cover art and overall design and to Norm Cohen for his help. The lingo was wrangled from Ramon F. Adams. Thanks to the University of Oklahoma for permission to use materials in *Come an' Get It: The Story of the Old Cowboy Cook* by Ramon F. Adams, copyright © 1952 by the University of Oklahoma Press and *Western Words: A Dictionary of the American West* by Ramon F. Adams, copyright © 1968 by the University of Oklahoma Press.

Cowboy Insult #25
He's as crooked as a snake in a cactus patch.